D1525069

healthy heart
recipes

Published by:
TRIDENT REFERENCE PUBLISHING
801 12th Avenue South, Suite 400
Naples, Fl 34102 USA

Tel: + 1 (239) 649-7077
www.tridentreference.com
email: sales@tridentreference.com

Healthy Heart Recipes
© TRIDENT REFERENCE PUBLISHING

Publisher
Simon St. John Bailey

Editor-in-chief
Susan Knightley

Prepress
Precision Prep & Press

Includes Index
ISBN 1582797293
UPC 6 15269 97293 9

Printed in The United States

introduction

If you are still doubtful about healthy food being
tasty, this book will persuade you! Do not waste
your time only on good intentions. Right away
start to look after your heart bearing in mind our
delicious proposals.

To modify eating habits and lifestyle is the clue
to prevent heart disease. This aim is within your

healthy heart recipes
introduction

reach if you accept the correct nutritious information and the delicious healthy selections that we offer you. Try our recipes and check their benefits.

- To diminish the intake of saturated fat, control the use of butter, cream, cold meat, sausages and cheese of high fat content.

- Avoid industrial products including hydrogenated vegetable oils which contain trans fats (the most harmful); such as cookies, buns, sweets, chocolates and breaded frozen products. Identify them by reading labels.

- Be sure you use a lot of fibers and antioxidants (vitamin C, betacarotenes, vitamin E, polyphenoles).This will be possible if you include in your daily menu lots of fruits and raw or slightly cooked vegetables of varied colors and if you choose whole cereals, pulses and tubers instead of products made with white flour.

- Choose extra virgin olive oil, avocados or nuts as a healthy vegetable fat source.

- Often replace meat by sea fish. Alternate lean white fish with blue fish providing good quality fat.

- Do away with or reduce to minimum the use of salt (sodium chloride) which increases blood pressure in sodium sensible individuals.

- Give priority to simple cooking methods (steam, microwave, boil, roast or grill), without any or very little fat.

- Reach and keep a healthy body weight, do not smoke and practice exercise daily and regularly; a 30 minutes' walk is enough if carried out methodical and constantly.

Difficulty scale

■□□I Easy to do

■■□I Requires attention

■■■I Requires experience

warm
seafood salad

■□□ | Cooking time: 10 minutes - Preparation time: 10 minutes

method

1. Arrange watercress and lettuce leaves on serving plates.
2. In a nonstick frying pan, heat oil and cook onion and garlic until soft. Add scallops, shrimp and fish and cook for 5-6 minutes or until shrimp turn pink and fish is just cooked. Season with pepper to taste. Arrange fish mixture over lettuce leaves.
3. To make dressing, combine lime juice, oil, pepper and dill in a screwtop jar and shake well to combine. Sprinkle over fish, garnish with dill sprigs and serve immediately.

....

Serves 6

Nutritional facts per serving
Calories: 172
Total fat: 6.5 g
Saturated fat: 0.9 g
Cholesterol: 116 mg
Fiber: 0.2 g

ingredients

> $1/2$ bunch watercress
> mignonette lettuce leaves
> butter lettuce leaves
> 1 tablespoon olive oil
> 1 onion, thinly sliced
> 1 clove garlic, crushed
> 250 g/8 oz scallops
> 250 g/8 oz shrimp, shelled and deveined
> 250 g/8 oz firm white fish fillets
> freshly ground black pepper
> fresh dill sprigs for garnish

dressing

> $1/2$ cup lime juice
> 1 tablespoon olive oil
> freshly ground black pepper
> 1 tablespoon finely chopped fresh dill

tip from the chef

In spite of its high cholesterol proportion, seafood is not dangerous for the heart because it has little total fat and a minimum of saturated fat.

green vegetable and pasta salad

■□□ | Cooking time: 15 minutes - Preparation time: 10 minutes

ingredients

> 250 g/8 oz dried green pasta spirals
> $1/3$ cup olive oil
> 210 g/7 oz green peas
> 125 g/4 oz green beans, halved
> 150 g/5 oz broccoli flowerets
> 2 small zucchini, sliced diagonally
> 2 tablespoons almonds
> 2 tablespoons freshly squeezed lemon juice
> 1 teaspoon French mustard
> 2 teaspoons chopped fresh tarragon

method

1. Cook pasta in boiling water until tender, drain, rinse under cold water and drain again. Place pasta in large bowl. Add 1 teaspoon oil, toss well.
2. Bring large pan of water to the boil. Add vegetables, cook for 30 seconds, drain. Rinse under cold water, drain again. Add to pasta.
3. Place almonds on oven tray, toast in moderate oven for 5 minutes, cool.
4. Combine remaining oil, lemon juice, mustard and tarragon, add to salad along with almonds. Refrigerate 2 hours before serving.

....

Serves 4

Nutritional facts per serving
Calories: 499
Total fat: 22.4 g
Saturated fat: 2 g
Cholesterol: 0
Fiber: 2.4 g

tip from the chef

Brief cooking helps vegetables keep antioxidant vitamins (betacarotenes and vitamin C).

chicken
and orange salad

■ □ □ | Cooking time: 0 minute - Preparation time: 15 minutes

method

1. In a large salad bowl gently mix chicken with celery, water chestnuts, orange segments and onion.
2. Combine parsley, oil, garlic and tarragon vinegar in a jar, shake well and pour over salad.

....
Serves 4

Nutritional facts per serving
Calories: 371
Total fat: 27.5 g
Saturated fat: 2.8 g
Cholesterol: 70 mg
Fiber: 0.6 g

ingredients

> 2 cups cooked skinless chicken breast, cut into bite-size pieces
> 1/2 cup celery, sliced
> 1/2 cup water chestnuts, cut in halves
> 1 cup orange segments
> 1 red onion, finely chopped
> 1 tablespoon chopped fresh parsley
> 1/3 cup olive oil
> 1 small clove garlic, crushed
> 3 tablespoons tarragon vinegar

tip from the chef

Soursweet combinations are attractive and they are welcome to do away with salt if necessary.

minted
green pea soup

■□□ | Cooking time: 25 minutes - Preparation time: 15 minutes

method

1. Heat oil in a saucepan. Cook onion for 2-3 minutes or until soft. Add stock, potato, lettuce, peas and mint and simmer for 20 minutes or until potato is tender. Season with pepper to taste. Set aside to cool.

2. Transfer soup mixture in batches to the bowl of a food processor or blender. Process until smooth. Chill for at least 2 hours before serving.

3. To serve, garnish with a tablespoon of yogurt, swirled through each bowl of soup, and a sprig of mint.

ingredients

> 1 tablespoon olive oil
> 1 onion, chopped
> 4 cups degreased chicken stock
> 1 large potato, diced
> 1/2 lettuce, shredded
> 500 g/1 lb frozen peas
> 1 tablespoon chopped fresh mint
> freshly ground black pepper
> 6 tablespoons low fat natural yogurt
> fresh mint sprigs for garnish

....
Serves 6

Nutritional facts per serving
Calories: 137
Total fat: 3 g
Saturated fat: 0.3 g
Cholesterol: 0.7 mg
Fiber: 2 g

tip from the chef

This soup is equally delicious served hot, accompanied with hot croûtons.

curried
pumpkin soup

■□□ I Cooking time: 25 minutes - Preparation time: 10 minutes

method

1. Heat oil in a large saucepan. Cook onion, coriander, cumin and chili powder until onion softens.
2. Stir pumpkin and stock into saucepan. Cook pumpkin for 20 minutes or until tender, then cool slightly. Transfer soup in batches to a food processor or blender and process until smooth.
3. Return soup to a clean saucepan and heat. Season to taste with pepper.

ingredients

> 1 tablespoon olive oil
> 1 large onion, chopped
> 1/2 teaspoon ground coriander
> 1/2 teaspoon ground cumin
> 1/2 teaspoon chili powder
> 3 cups cubed pumpkin
> 4 cups degreased chicken stock
> freshly ground black pepper

....
Serves 4

Nutritional facts per serving
Calories: 93
Total fat: 3.8 g
Saturated fat: 0.4 g
Cholesterol: 0
Fiber: 0.9 g

tip from the chef

The use of olive oil for shallow frying secures a higher resistance to temperatures avoiding aggressive compounds to be formed.

chilled
tomato soup

a

■□□ | Cooking time: 10 minutes - Preparation time: 15 minutes

method

1. Heat oil in a large saucepan. Cook onion and garlic for 2-3 minutes or until onion softens. Add stock and mint, simmer for 5 minutes. Set aside to cool.
2. Place tomatoes and stock mixture in a food processor or blender (a) and process until soup is smooth. Stir in zucchini (b) and season with pepper to taste. Refrigerate until well chilled.
3. To make tomato ice cubes, place a mint leaf in each space of an ice cube tray. Mix together tomato juice and water, pour into tray (c). Freeze.
4. To serve, place ice cubes in each soup bowl and pour chilled soup over.

ingredients

> 1 tablespoon olive oil
> 1 onion, chopped
> 1 clove garlic, crushed
> 4 cups vegetable stock
> 4 tablespoons finely chopped fresh mint
> 450 g/15 oz canned tomatoes
> 2 zucchini, coarsely grated
> freshly ground black pepper

tomato ice cubes

> fresh mint leaves
> 3/4 cup tomato juice
> 3/4 cup water

....
Serves 4

Nutritional facts per serving
Calories: 92
Total fat: 4 g
Saturated fat: 0.4 g
Cholesterol: 0
Fiber: 1.1 g

tip from the chef

Start any dinner party with this easy-to-make refreshing summer soup, and no one will guess just how few calories there are in it! Besides it is particularly rich in lycopene, an excellent phytonutrient acting as an antioxidant which increases the defense mechanism.

b

c

layered
lunch loaf

■ □ □ | Cooking time: 0 minute - Preparation time: 15 minutes

ingredients

> 1 x 450 g/15 oz round rye or wholegrain cottage loaf

mixed sprouts layer
> 2 teaspoons tomato paste (purée)
> 4 tablespoons low fat natural yogurt
> 1 teaspoon ground coriander
> 90 g/3 oz alfalfa sprouts
> 60 g/2 oz bean sprouts
> 90 g/3 oz snow pea sprouts or watercress

roast beef layer
> 3 teaspoons French mustard
> 4 slices lean rare roast beef
> 4 lettuce leaves of your choice
> 1/2 red pepper, chopped

tomato salad layer
> 2 tomatoes, sliced
> 3 gherkins, sliced
> 1/2 cucumber, sliced

method

1. Cut bread horizontally into four even layers.
2. For sprouts layer, place tomato paste (purée), yogurt and coriander in a bowl and mix to combine. Place alfalfa sprouts, bean sprouts and snow pea sprouts or watercress on bottom layer of bread. Top with yogurt mixture and second bread layer.
3. For beef layer, spread bread with mustard, then top with roast beef, lettuce and red pepper and third bread layer.
4. For salad layer, top bread with tomatoes, gherkins and cucumber and final bread layer. Serve cut into wedges.

....
Serves 4

Nutritional facts per serving
Calories: 547
Total fat: 11.9 g
Saturated fat: 2.9 g
Cholesterol: less than 1 mg
Fiber: 2.6 g

tip from the chef
If you are making this for a packed lunch, wrap each wedge in plastic food wrap.
In place of the roast beef you could use roast lean chicken, turkey or lamb. Other attractive options are canned tuna or salmon in brine or springwater.

tomato
and cucumber on rye

■□□ | Cooking time: 0 minute - Preparation time: 15 minutes

method

1. In a bowl combine tomatoes, cucumber, green pepper, green onions and celery.
2. To make dressing, combine vinegar, oil, mustard, chili and black pepper to taste in a screw top jar. Shake well to combine and pour over tomato salad.
3. Divide watercress between bread slices and top with tomato salad.

Makes 4

Nutritional facts per serving
Calories: 147
Total fat: 5 g
Saturated fat: 0.4 g
Cholesterol: 0
Fiber: 1.5 g

ingredients

> **2 tomatoes, thinly sliced**
> **1/2 cucumber, thinly sliced**
> **1/2 green pepper, diced**
> **3 green onions, thinly sliced**
> **1 stalk celery, chopped**
> **1/2 bunch watercress**
> **4 slices rye bread**

dressing

> **3 tablespoons white wine vinegar**
> **1 tablespoon olive oil**
> **1/2 teaspoon mustard powder**
> **pinch chili powder**
> **freshly ground black pepper**

tip from the chef

This sophisticated vegetarian sandwich is highly advisable due to the quality of its fats and its minimum tenor of saturated fat. Any kind of bread made of whole cereals or seeds and cereals can be used.

SOY burgers

■□□ I Cooking time: 15 minutes - Preparation time: 20 minutes

ingredients
> **6 multigrain rolls, split and toasted**
> **lettuce leaves and tomato slices**
> **30 g/1 oz alfalfa sprouts**
> **1 raw beetroot, grated**
> **4 tablespoons sunflower seeds, toasted**

minted soy burgers
> **440 g/14 oz canned soy beans, rinsed and drained**
> **1 cup/60 g/2 oz wholemeal breadcrumbs, made from stale bread**
> **1 red onion, finely chopped**
> **1 carrot, grated**
> **3 tablespoons besan flour**
> **3 tablespoons chopped fresh mint**
> **1 egg, lightly beaten**
> **75 g/2^1/2 oz sesame seeds**
> **2 tablespoons olive oil**

creamy dressing
> **1 cup/200 g/6^1/2 oz low fat natural yogurt**
> **1 tablespoon chopped fresh coriander**
> **1 tablespoon grated fresh ginger**
> **2 tablespoons sweet chili sauce**
> **1 clove garlic, crushed**
> **freshly ground black pepper**

method
1. To make dressing, mix all ingredients in a bowl.
2. To make burgers, roughly chop soy beans in a food processor or blender. Combine beans, breadcrumbs, onion, carrot, flour, mint and egg (a). Shape mixture into 6 burgers and roll in sesame seeds (b). Heat oil in a frying pan over a medium heat, add burgers and cook for 6 minutes each side (c) or until golden.
3. Top bottom half of each roll with lettuce, tomato, a burger, a few alfalfa sprouts, beetroot, sunflower seeds, a spoonful of dressing and top half of roll.

....
Serves 6

Nutritional facts per serving
Calories: 471
Total fat: 19 g
Saturated fat: 2.2 g
Cholesterol: 34 mg
Fiber: 3.2 g

tip from the chef
Besan flour is made from chickpeas and is available from Asian and healthy food stores.

a   b   c

zucchini bake

■ □ □ ∣ Cooking time: 20 minutes - Preparation time: 15 minutes

method

1. Heat oil in a saucepan and cook onion, garlic, green pepper and herbs for 2-3 minutes or until onion is soft. Add mushrooms and cook for 5 minutes.
2. Stir in tomatoes and tomato paste, cook until mixture boils. Stir in cornflour mixture and cook until sauce thickens.
3. Boil, steam or microwave zucchini until just tender. Place in a shallow ovenproof dish and pour tomato sauce over. Top with breadcrumbs and cheese.
4. Place under a preheated grill for 5 minutes or until top is golden.

....
Serves 4

Nutritional facts per serving
Calories: 169
Total fat: 6.2 g
Saturated fat: 1.4 g
Cholesterol: 5 mg
Fiber: 2.5 g

ingredients

> 1 tablespoon olive oil
> 2 large onions, sliced into rings
> 1 clove garlic, crushed
> 1 green pepper, diced
> 1 teaspoon mixed Italian herbs
> 125 g/4 oz mushrooms, sliced
> 450 g/15 oz canned tomatoes, undrained and mashed
> 1 tablespoon tomato paste (purée)
> 1 tablespoon cornflour blended with $1/2$ cup water
> 3 medium zucchini, thickly sliced

topping

> $1/2$ cup fresh breadcrumbs
> 2 tablespoons grated cheese

tip from the chef

Choose a low fat cheese and check grill temperature to avoid fat to be altered.

tuscan
vegetable terrine

■□□ | Cooking time: 30 minutes - Preparation time: 20 minutes

ingredients

> 1 bunch/180 g/6 oz rocket

vegetable terrine

> 300 g/10 oz pumpkin, peeled
> 16 Italian tomatoes
> 400 g/13½ oz low fat bocconcini cheese, well drained
> 1 bunch/50 g/1½ oz fresh basil
> freshly ground black pepper

mustard and balsamic dressing

> 1 teaspoon wholegrain mustard
> 2 tablespoons balsamic vinegar
> 2 tablespoons olive oil

method

1. Line a terrine dish with plastic food wrap, leaving enough wrap overhanging the sides to cover top of terrine. Set aside.
2. To make terrine, cut pumpkin into 1 cm/½ in thick slices. Place on a baking tray. Lightly brush with olive oil. Bake at a 180°C/350°F/Gas 4 for 20-30 minutes or until cooked, but still firm. Cool.
3. Cut tomatoes in half lengthwise. Remove seeds and press gently to flatten. Cut cheese into 6 mm/¼ in thick slices.
4. Layer the ingredients in the terrine in the following order: tomatoes, basil, cheese, tomatoes, basil, cheese, pumpkin, basil, tomatoes, cheese, basil, tomatoes and finally cheese; place tomatoes skin side down and season with pepper. Cover terrine with the overhanging plastic wrap. Weigh down. Refrigerate overnight.
5. To make dressing, place mustard, vinegar and oil in a screwtop jar. Shake well.
6. Using the plastic wrap, carefully lift terrine. Cut into thick slices. Line serving plates with rocket leaves. Place a slice on top. Drizzle with dressing.

Serves 8-10

tip from the chef

For something different, replace mozzarella for firm tofu, and the dressing for basil blended with drops of lemon juice and olive oil.

Nutritional facts per serving
Calories: 204
Total fat: 11.3 g
Saturated fat: 1.6 g
Cholesterol: 8 mg
Fiber: 1 g

vegetable strudel

■□□ | Cooking time: 40 minutes - Preparation time: 15 minutes

method

1. Steam or microwave broccoli and cauliflower until just tender, drain.

2. Heat oil in a saucepan, cook onion for 5 minutes. Add combined cornflour, milk and nutmeg. Cook until sauce boils and thickens. Remove from heat, stir in mozzarella cheese. Add cooked broccoli and cauliflower (a), mix well.

3. Layer filo pastry sheets on top of each other. Brush lightly with extra oil between each sheet (b).

4. Place filling down the long edge of pastry, leaving a 5 cm/2 in border on sides and front. Fold sides in and roll up (c).

5. Brush strudel with oil. Place onto oiled oven tray. Bake in moderately hot oven for 30 minutes. Serve cut into thick slices.

ingredients

> 3 cups broccoli flowerets
> 3 cups cauliflower flowerets
> 1 teaspoon olive oil
> 1 onion, finely chopped
> 1 tablespoon cornflour
> 1 cup skim milk
> pinch ground nutmeg
> 60 g/2 oz low fat mozzarella cheese, grated
> 8 sheets filo pastry
> 2 tablespoons olive oil, extra

Serves 4

Nutritional facts per serving
Calories: 565
Total fat: 25 g
Saturated fat: 4.6 g
Cholesterol: 9 mg
Fiber: 2.1 g

tip from the chef

Cauliflower and broccoli belong to the cruciferous family, vegetables rich in fibers and in antioxidants (vitamin C and betacarotenes).

fettuccine
with spicy seafood sauce

■□□ | Cooking time: 50 minutes - Preparation time: 15 minutes

method

1. Cook pasta according to package directions. Drain and keep warm.

2. To make sauce, heat oil in a saucepan. Cook onion, pepper, garlic, chili, cumin and coriander until onion softens. Add tomatoes, wine and tomato paste. Cook over medium heat for 30 minutes longer, or until sauce reduces and thickens.

3. Add squid and cook for 5 minutes or until just tender. Add mussels and shrimp and cook for 4-5 minutes. Mix in 2 tablespoons coriander. Pour sauce over pasta and serve garnished with remaining coriander.

....
Serves 4

Nutritional facts per serving
Calories: 655
Total fat: 6.9 g
Saturated fat: 0.8 g
Cholesterol: 226 mg
Fiber: 1.2 g

ingredients
> **500 g/1 lb mixed colored fettuccine**

spicy seafood sauce
> **1 tablespoon olive oil**
> **1 onion, sliced**
> **1 red pepper, diced**
> **1 clove garlic, crushed**
> **1 red chili, seeded and finely chopped**
> **1/2 teaspoon ground cumin**
> **1/2 teaspoon ground coriander**
> **450 g/15 oz canned tomatoes, undrained and mashed**
> **3 tablespoons dry white wine**
> **1 tablespoon tomato paste (purée)**
> **125 g/4 oz squid rings**
> **125 g/4 oz mussels, scrubbed and beards removed**
> **500 g/1 lb shrimp, peeled and deveined**
> **4 tablespoons finely chopped fresh coriander**

tip from the chef

In this complete dish with a low saturated fat content we obtain a good flavor through the use of spices that allow not to add salt. Accompany with a salad made of your favorite vegetables, or try combining raw spinach, orange segments, thinly sliced mushrooms and shallots.

pasta
with herb sauce

■□□ | Cooking time: 15 minutes - Preparation time: 10 minutes

ingredients

> 500 g/1 lb mixed colored spiral pasta

herb sauce

> 1 tablespoon olive oil
> 1 small onion, chopped
> 1 clove garlic, crushed
> 2 tablespoons flour
> 1/2 cup vegetable stock
> 1 cup low fat natural yogurt
> 2 tablespoons finely chopped fresh parsley
> 2 tablespoons finely chopped fresh basil
> 2 tablespoons finely chopped fresh chives
> freshly ground black pepper

method

1. Cook pasta according to package directions. Drain and keep warm.
2. To make sauce, heat oil in a saucepan and cook onion and garlic for 2-3 minutes. Stir in flour and stock and continue to cook until sauce thickens.
3. Stir in yogurt and heat gently. Mix in parsley, basil and chives. Season with pepper to taste.
4. Spoon sauce over pasta and serve garnished with additional fresh herbs if desired.

....
Serves 4

Nutritional facts per serving

Calories: 515
Total fat: 5.1 g
Saturated fat: 0.4 g
Cholesterol: 3 mg
Fiber: 0.1 g

tip from the chef

This sauce is also great poured over steamed vegetables. You can use it as an original alternative to cream and white sauce. While pasta is cooking on the stovetop, you can make sauce in the microwave. Place oil, onion and garlic in a microwave-safe jug; cook on High (100%) for 2 minutes. Stir in flour and stock. Cook on High (100%) for 2 minutes, until sauce thickens. Add yogurt; cook on Medium (50%) for 2 minutes, until just heated through. Mix in herbs and season with black pepper to taste.

spaghetti
with ratatouille sauce

■□□ | Cooking time: 50 minutes - Preparation time: 10 minutes

method

1. Cook pasta according to package directions. Drain and keep warm.
2. To make sauce, place eggplant, onion. garlic, green pepper, zucchini, tomatoes, wine, basil, thyme, oregano and black pepper to taste in a nonstick frying pan. Cook over low heat for 30-45 minutes, stirring occasionally.
3. Spoon sauce over pasta and serve sprinkled with a little grated Parmesan cheese.

....
Serves 4

Nutritional facts per serving
Calories: 520
Total fat: 2.2 g
Saturated fat: 0.25 g
Cholesterol: 2 mg
Fiber: 2.5 g

ingredients
> **500 g/1 lb wholemeal spaghetti**

ratatouille sauce
> 1 eggplant, diced
> 1 large onion, sliced
> 1 clove garlic, crushed
> 1 green pepper, diced
> 2 zucchini, diced
> 500 g/1 lb tomatoes, peeled and roughly chopped
> 1/2 cup dry white wine
> 1 tablespoon finely chopped fresh basil
> 1/2 teaspoon dried thyme
> 1/2 teaspoon dried oregano
> freshly ground black pepper
> 2 tablespoons grated Parmesan cheese

tip from the chef
The combination of pasta and vegetables saves fat and add fiber, which is good for a healthy heart.
You can also eat this delicious and versatile ratatouille on its own, hot or cold.

lemon
fish parcels

■□□ | Cooking time: 20 minutes - Preparation time: 15 minutes

ingredients
> 4 large white fish fillets
> 1 tablespoon finely chopped capers
> 1/2 cup lemon juice
> freshly ground black pepper
> 8 fresh or canned asparagus spears
> 1/2 teaspoon paprika

method
1. Lightly grease 4 sheets of aluminum foil and place a fish fillet in the center of each sheet.
2. Top each fillet with a teaspoon of capers. Pour over lemon juice and season with pepper to taste. Place two asparagus spears over each fillet and dust lightly with paprika.
3. Fold up edges of aluminum foil and completely encase fish. Place parcels on an oven tray and bake at 180°C/350°F/Gas 4 for 15-20 minutes, or until fish flakes when tested with a fork. Remove from parcels to serve.

....
Serves 4

Nutritional facts per serving
Calories: 187
Total fat: 1.2 g
Saturated fat: 0.4 g
Cholesterol: 120 mg
Fiber: 0.3 g

tip from the chef
Because of its low fat content and its excellent proteins, fish is good for the heart. If you use blue fish (mackerel, tuna) instead of white fish, you will obtain more calories and fat, but with a great addition of omega 3. You can use either aluminum foil or greaseproof paper to make these parcels.

teriyaki fish

■□□ | Cooking time: 10 minutes - Preparation time: 10 minutes

method

1. To make marinade, combine teriyaki sauce, honey, sherry, ginger and garlic.
2. Place fish fillets in a single layer in a shallow dish. Pour marinade over fish. Cover and marinate for 1 hour.
3. Place sesame seeds in a frying pan and cook over medium heat until golden brown, stirring frequently.
4. Remove fish from marinade and grill for 2-3 minutes on each side. Baste occasionally with marinade during cooking. Serve sprinkled with sesame seeds.

ingredients

> **4 large firm white fish fillets**
> **2 teaspoons sesame seeds**

marinade

> **3 tablespoons teriyaki sauce**
> **1 tablespoon honey**
> **1 tablespoon dry sherry**
> **1/4 teaspoon grated fresh ginger**
> **1 clove garlic, crushed**

....
Serves 4

Nutritional facts per serving
Calories: 199
Total fat: 2.2 g
Saturated fat: 0.5 g
Cholesterol: 120 mg
Fiber: 0.1 g

tip from the chef

Fish cooks very quickly under the grill. Remember to turn halfway through cooking time. For best results, preheat grill. The heat of the grill and the thickness of the fish will determine cooking time.

orange chicken

■□□ | Cooking time: 35 minutes - Preparation time: 10 minutes

ingredients

> **4 boneless chicken breast fillets**
> **2 teaspoons cornflour blended with 3 tablespoons degreased chicken stock**

marinade

> **3/4 cup orange juice**
> **1 tablespoon grated orange rind**
> **1/2 teaspoon French mustard**
> **1/2 teaspoon ground nutmeg**
> **1/2 teaspoon curry powder**
> **freshly ground black pepper**

method

1. To make marinade, combine orange juice, rind, mustard, nutmeg and curry powder in a shallow glass dish. Season with pepper to taste. Add chicken and marinate for 1-2 hours.
2. Transfer chicken and a little of the marinade to a baking dish. Bake at 180°C/350°F/Gas 4 for 30 minutes, or until chicken is tender.
3. Place remaining marinade and cornflour mixture in a saucepan. Cook over medium heat until sauce boils and thickens. Spoon over chicken and serve.

....

Serves 4

<u>Nutritional facts per serving</u>
Calories: 209
Total fat: 3 g
Saturated fat: 0.9 g
Cholesterol: 140 mg
Fiber: 0

tip from the chef

This recipe lacks fibers. Do not forget to include raw salads and fruit in the same meal.

chili chicken

■□□ | Cooking time: 40 minutes - Preparation time: 12 minutes

method

1. Heat a nonstick frying pan over a medium heat. Add chicken and cook for 4 minutes each side or until brown.
2. Add tomatoes, zucchini, red pepper, green or yellow pepper, spring onions, wine and chili sauce to pan and bring to simmering.
3. Cover and simmer, stirring occasionally, for 30 minutes or until chicken is tender and sauce reduces and thickens.

....
Serves 4

ingredients

> 4 x 125 g/4 oz boneless chicken breast fillets, sliced
> 2 x 440 g/14 oz canned tomatoes, undrained and crushed
> 2 zucchini, sliced
> 1 red pepper, sliced
> 1 green or yellow pepper, sliced
> 4 spring onions, sliced
> 1/2 cup/125 ml/4 fl oz dry white wine
> 1 tablespoon chili sauce

Nutritional facts per serving
Calories: 213
Total fat: 2.6 g
Saturated fat: 0.6 g
Cholesterol: 87 mg
Fiber: 3.5 g

tip from the chef

This recipe –very helpful to add fibers to the menu– can also be made with turkey breast. If you wish, serve with brown rice.

stir-fry chicken with cashews

■□□ | Cooking time: 15 minutes - Preparation time: 15 minutes

ingredients
> 1 tablespoon olive oil
> 1 red onion, cut into petals
> 1 carrot, sliced diagonally
> 1 clove garlic, crushed
> 1 teaspoon grated fresh ginger
> 375 g/³/₄ lb boneless chicken breast fillets, cut into strips
> 2 teaspoons olive oil, extra
> 250 g/8 oz broccoli, cut into flowerets
> 2 tablespoons cashews
> ¹/₂ cup degreased chicken stock
> 3 spring onions, sliced diagonally
> 2 teaspoons cornflour
> 2 teaspoons tamari or soy sauce
> 1 tablespoon sherry
> ¹/₄ teaspoon sesame oil

method
1. Heat oil in a frying pan, cook onion and carrot for 5 minutes. Add garlic and ginger, cook for 1 minute longer. Remove from pan.
2. Add chicken in batches to pan, cook until lightly browned. Remove from pan.
3. Heat extra oil in pan, cook broccoli and cashews until cashews are lightly browned.
4. Return vegetables and chicken to pan. Add stock, spring onions and combined cornflour, tamari or soy sauce, sherry and sesame oil. Cook until mixture boils and thickens.

....
Serves 4

Nutritional facts per serving
Calories: 253
Total fat: 12 g
Saturated fat: 1.7 g
Cholesterol: 66 mg
Fiber: 2 g

tip from the chef
Olive oil and dried fruits are a reliable contribution of mono-unsaturated fatty acids, thus benefiting heart health.
Tamari (Japanese soy sauce) is available at healthy food shops, Oriental food stores and some supermarkets.

veal goulash

■□□ | Cooking time: 30 minutes - Preparation time: 15 minutes

method

1. Trim meat of all visible fat and cut into 2.5 cm/1 in cubes (a). Place paprika, flour and pepper to taste in a plastic bag; add meat and shake (b) to coat evenly. Shake off excess flour mixture.
2. Heat oil in a large saucepan, cook onion and garlic for 2-3 minutes or until soft.
3. Combine tomato paste, wine and stock, pour into pan. Add meat (c). Bring to the boil, then reduce heat and simmer, covered, for 20-25 minutes or until meat is tender.
4. Remove from heat and stir in yogurt. Serve sprinkled with parsley.

....
Serves 4

Nutritional facts per serving
Calories: 245
Total fat: 11 g
Saturated fat: 2 g
Cholesterol: 100 mg
Fiber: 2.5 g

ingredients

> 4 x 125 g/4 oz lean veal steaks
> 1¹/2 tablespoons paprika
> 2 tablespoons flour
> freshly ground black pepper
> 2 teaspoons olive oil
> 2 onions, chopped
> 1 clove garlic, crushed
> 1 tablespoon tomato paste (purée)
> 3 tablespoons dry red wine
> ¹/2 cup degreased beef stock
> 3 tablespoons low fat natural yogurt
> 1 tablespoon finely chopped fresh parsley

tip from the chef

Try adding low fat natural yogurt to meat recipes which list sour cream at the end, but remember not to boil after adding or it will curdle.

a

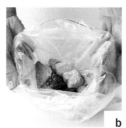

b

c

pork with
prunes and apricot

■□□ I Cooking time: 20 minutes - Preparation time: 15 minutes

ingredients

> 2 tablespoons olive oil
> 500 g/1 lb lean pork, cubed
> 1 onion, cut into eighths
> 1/2 teaspoon dried sage
> 1/2 teaspoon dried thyme
> 1 cup apple juice
> 10 large pitted prunes
> 1 teaspoon cider vinegar
> 8 dried apricots
> 2 tablespoons slivered almonds, toasted

method

1. Heat oil in a frying pan. Cook pork, onion, sage and thyme until meat changes color and is just tender.
2. Purée apple juice, six prunes and vinegar in a food processor or blender and pour into pan. Stir in apricots and remaining prunes.
3. Cook, covered, for 15 minutes, stirring occasionally. Serve sprinkled with almonds.

....
Serves 4

Nutritional facts per serving
Calories: 418
Total fat: 22 g
Saturated fat: 4.1 g
Cholesterol: 81 mg
Fiber: 1 g

tip from the chef

With today's leaner cuts of meat, you can still enjoy a juicy roast, but remember to keep meat portions moderate. As a rule, 500 g/1 lb meat will serve 4 people for dinner, as would four small chops or four chicken breasts. This is equivalent to about 125 g/1/4 pound meat or chicken per person –sufficient to supply all necessary iron, protein and B vitamins.

fresh figs with orange and grand marnier

■□□ | Cooking time: 0 minute - Preparation time: 15 minutes

method

1. Cut stalks off figs and cut figs into quarters. Place in a medium bowl.
2. Pour over orange juice and Grand Marnier. Cover, refrigerate overnight.
3. Serve chilled figs and marinade in glass individual dishes or tall glasses.

ingredients

> **12 slightly under-ripe green or purple figs**
> **1 cup fresh orange juice**
> **1/4 cup Grand Marnier**

....
Serves 4

Nutritional facts per serving
Calories: 129
Total fat: 1 g
Saturated fat: 0.3 g
Cholesterol: 0
Fiber: 1.5 g

tip from the chef

Figs enrich food value with sugar and soluble fiber. A small quantity of Grand Marnier is enough to give them a delicious aroma.

blueberry
and apple crunch

■□□ I Cooking time: 20 minutes - Preparation time: 10 minutes

ingredients
> **360 g/12 oz canned blueberries, drained**
> **360 g/12 oz canned unsweetened apple slices, drained**
> **2 teaspoons grated lemon rind**
> **1 tablespoon butter, melted**
> **1 tablespoon brown sugar**
> **1 1/2 cups cornflakes**
> **1 tablespoon sesame seeds**

method
1. Combine blueberries, apples and lemon rind and spoon into an ovenproof dish.
2. Mix together butter, sugar and cornflakes and spread over apple mixture in dish. Sprinkle sesame seeds over.
3. Bake at 180°C/350°F/Gas 4 for 20 minutes or until golden brown.

....
Serves 6

Nutritional facts per serving
Calories: 126
Total fat: 2.6 g
Saturated fat: 1.3 g
Cholesterol: 6 mg
Fiber: 2 g

tip from the chef
Strictly use only the quantity of butter the recipe calls for. Be moderate when eating butter, as it is rich in saturated fat and cholesterol.
You can use fresh or frozen blueberries instead of canned ones.

ginger
melon salad

■□□ | Cooking time: 0 minute - Preparation time: 10 minutes

method

1. Halve melons and remove seeds. Scoop out flesh with a melon baller. Place balls in a glass serving dish.
2. Sprinkle sugar over and drizzle with Grand Marnier. Toss lightly.
3. Garnish with finely chopped candied ginger and chill before serving.

ingredients

> 3 melons (cantaloupe, honeydew, watermelon), each about 500 g/1 lb
> 2 tablespoons superfine sugar
> 2 tablespoons Grand Marnier
> 4 pieces candied ginger

....
Serves 6

Nutritional facts per serving
Calories: 135
Total fat: 1.6 g
Saturated fat: 0.6 g
Cholesterol: 0
Fiber: 1.2 g

tip from the chef

Save time by storing melons in the refrigerator when you buy them. You will then be able to serve a chilled salad immediately.

mango mousse

■□□ | Cooking time: 0 minute - Preparation time: 15 minutes

ingredients

> **2 mangoes, peeled and stoned**
> **1 tablespoon sugar**
> **2 tablespoons gelatin**
> **1/4 cup water**
> **3/4 cup evaporated skim milk**

method

1. Blend or process mangoes until smooth. Combine sugar and mango purée in a bowl.
2. Sprinkle gelatin over water, dissolve over hot water, add to mango mixture.
3. Beat milk in a small bowl until frothy, fold into mango mixture.
4. Pour into serving glasses, refrigerate until set.

....
Serves 4

Nutritional facts per serving
Calories: 136
Total fat: 0.6 g
Saturated fat: 0.1 g
Cholesterol: 2 mg
Fiber: 1 g

tip from the chef
Mango slices and halved strawberries can be used as a decoration for this delicious mousse rich in antioxidants (betacarotenes and vitamin C).

pecan crispies

■ □ □ | Cooking time: 3 minutes - Preparation time: 15 minutes

method

1. Beat egg whites in a large bowl with an electric mixer until soft peaks form.
2. Add salt, vanilla essence and sugar, beat for a further 1 minute, fold in nuts.
3. Drop teaspoons of mixture onto a greaseproof paper lined baking tray.
4. Bake in moderate oven for 2-3 minutes, turn off oven and leave biscuits in oven for 1 hour.
5. Use a spatula to ease biscuits off paper, store in an airtight container.

ingredients

> **3 egg whites**
> **pinch salt**
> **1 teaspoon vanilla essence**
> **3/4 cup caster sugar**
> **2 cups pecan nuts, chopped**

Serves 10 (makes about 40)

Nutritional facts per serving
Calories: 56
Total fat: 3.4 g
Saturated fat: 0.3 g
Cholesterol: 0
Fiber: 0.1 g

tip from the chef

One serving of these crispies is equivalent in calories to a small fruit and provides a moderate fat contribution, mostly composed by unsaturated fat.

spicy apple cake

■□□ | Cooking time: 35 minutes - Preparation time: 15 minutes

method

1. Combine oil and sugar in a large bowl. Whisk in eggs and vanilla.
2. Combine flour and spice in one bowl and apples, lemon rind and sultanas in another. Fold flour mixture and apple mixture alternately into beaten egg mixture.
3. Spoon mixture into a greased and lined 22.5 cm/9 in ring tin and bake at 180°C/350°F/Gas 4 for 30-35 minutes or until cooked when tested with a skewer.
4. Stand 5 minutes before turning out on a wire rack to cool.

Serves 12

ingredients

> 3 tablespoons olive oil
> 3/4 cup superfine sugar
> 2 eggs, lightly beaten
> 1 teaspoon vanilla essence
> 1 cup self-rising flour, sifted
> 1 1/2 teaspoons apple pie spice
> 360 g/12 oz canned unsweetened apple slices, drained
> 1 teaspoon grated lemon rind
> 1/2 cup sultanas

Nutritional facts per serving
Calories: 181
Total fat: 5.3 g
Saturated fat: 0.7 g
Cholesterol: 33 mg
Fiber: 0.3 g

tip from the chef

This cake, low in saturated fat, can also be made with pears or peaches and covered with icing sugar blended with drops of lemon juice.

hazelnut torte

a

■□□ | Cooking time: 35 minutes - Preparation time: 15 minutes

method

1. Beat egg whites until soft peaks form. Add sugar a spoonful at a time, beating well after each addition, and continue beating until meringue is thick and glossy.
2. Whisk egg yolks until light and fluffy, then stir in combined hazelnuts, cracker crumbs, baking powder, orange rind and almond essence (a). Fold meringue into hazelnut mixture (b).
3. Spoon mixture into a lightly greased and lined 22.5 cm/9 in springform cake tin (c). Bake at 180°C/350°F/Gas 4 for 30-35 minutes. Stand 5 minutes before turning out on a wire rack to cool.
4. Decorate top of cake with strawberries and dust with icing sugar.

ingredients

> 4 egg whites
> 3 tablespoons superfine sugar
> 3 egg yolks
> 1/2 cup ground hazelnuts
> 4 tablespoons water cracker crumbs
> 1/2 teaspoon baking powder
> 1 teaspoon grated orange rind
> 1/4 teaspoon almond essence
> 1 cup strawberries, hulled
> 1 teaspoon icing sugar

....
Serves 8

Nutritional facts per serving
Calories: 132
Total fat: 7.3 g
Saturated fat: 1.6 g
Cholesterol: 75 mg
Fiber: 0.5 g

tip from the chef

One serving of this torte contains the same quantity of sugar as a small fruit, their fat mostly being unsaturated. Thus, it is a healthy preparation. To enhance the taste of hazelnuts, dry in the oven until crispy before grinding.

b

c

index